Jackie Robinson Changes the Game

Karen Davila

Boston, Massachusetts
Chandler, Arizona
Glenview, Illinois
Upper Saddle River, New Jersey

Illustrations
All illustrations: London Ladd.

ISBN-13: 978-0-328-67563-0
ISBN-10: 0-328-67563-6

5 6 V0FL 16 15 14 13

Jackie Robinson loved sports. He played on many school teams.

Jackie Robinson liked to jump. But he loved baseball even more.

Major League teams would not let African Americans play. It was not fair.

Then one team made a change. That team let Jackie Robinson play.

Some people tried to stop Robinson.
He had to try even harder.

Robinson led the way for others. He was a **champion** in baseball and in **equal rights**.

Glossary

champion someone who is the best at something

equal rights freedom to do what other people do

Major League main group of teams in baseball